RAND CORPORATION

The Hurricane Sandy Rebuilding Task Force's Infrastructure Resilience Guidelines

An Initial Assessment of Implementation by Federal Agencies

Melissa L. Finucane, Noreen Clancy, Henry H. Willis, Debra Knopman

Prepared for the U.S. Department of Homeland Security

For more information on this publication, visit www.rand.org/t/RR841

Library of Congress Cataloging-in-Publication Data is available for this publication.
ISBN: 978-0-8330-8826-0

Published by the RAND Corporation, Santa Monica, Calif.

Cover photo: A bulldozer is parked in the Queens borough of New York. A concrete foundation, center, is all that remains of a house that burned to the ground during Superstorm Sandy in October 2012 (AP/Mark Lennihan).

Preface

In the spring and summer of 2013, the Presidential Hurricane Sandy Rebuilding Task Force (established through Executive Order 13632) developed its Infrastructure Resilience Guidelines to ensure that federal agencies incorporate key principles of resilience into their formulation, evaluation, and prioritization of infrastructure investments related to Sandy rebuilding. To assess the potential effects of the guidelines, the U.S. Department of Homeland Security sponsored a study by the RAND Corporation to assess federal agencies' implementation of the guidelines. This report briefly summarizes the study's results, drawing on interviews and documents from federal agencies, state and local governments, and nongovernmental organizations. We describe implementation processes and highlight lessons learned. The findings will be of interest to policymakers in federal, state, and local agencies and to other organizations and individuals engaged in activities and initiatives to enhance the resilience of U.S. infrastructure.

The RAND Homeland Security and Defense Center

The research reported here was conducted in the RAND Homeland Security and Defense Center (HSDC) under contract No. W91WAW-12-C-0030. Center projects examine a wide range of risk-management problems, including coastal and border security, emergency preparedness and response, defense support to civil authorities, transportation security, domestic intelligence, and technology acquisition. Center clients include the U.S. Department of Homeland

Security, the U.S. Department of Defense, the U.S. Department of Justice, and other organizations charged with security and disaster preparedness, response, and recovery.

HSDC is a joint center of two research divisions: RAND Justice, Infrastructure, and Environment and the RAND National Security Research Division. RAND Justice, Infrastructure, and Environment is dedicated to improving policy and decisionmaking in a wide range of policy domains, including civil and criminal justice, infrastructure protection and homeland security, transportation and energy policy, and environmental and natural resource policy. The RAND National Security Research Division conducts research and analysis for all national security sponsors other than the U.S. Air Force and the Army. The division includes the National Defense Research Institute, a federally funded research and development center whose sponsors include the Office of the Secretary of Defense, the Joint Staff, the Unified Combatant Commands, the defense agencies, and the U.S. Department of the Navy. The National Security Research Division also conducts research for the U.S. intelligence community and the ministries of defense of U.S. allies and partners.

Questions or comments about this report should be sent to the project leaders, Melissa Finucane (Melissa_Finucane@rand.org) and Henry Willis (Henry_Willis@rand.org). For more information about the Homeland Security and Defense Center, see http://www.rand.org/hsdc or contact the director at hsdc@rand.org.

Contents

Tables

Summary

In October 2012, Hurricane Sandy struck the East Coast of the United States, devastating communities across the region. This disaster motivated the federal government to examine how it might improve community and infrastructure resilience so that communities are better prepared for existing and future threats, including those exacerbated by climate change. Resilience involves enabling a region to withstand the effects of a disaster, respond effectively, recover quickly, adapt to changing conditions, and manage future disaster risk over time.

To ensure that federal agencies incorporate key principles of resilience into their formulation, evaluation, and prioritization of infrastructure investments related to Sandy rebuilding, the Presidential Hurricane Sandy Rebuilding Task Force developed its Infrastructure Resilience Guidelines in the spring and summer of 2013.[1] The aims of the guidelines are to (1) ensure that federal agencies have a consistent approach to building resilience and (2) improve decisionmaking to better protect communities and to ensure wise investment of scarce public resources by setting criteria for investment and by helping align projects with national policy goals. The seven principles in the guidelines are

1. comprehensive analysis
2. transparent and inclusive decision processes

[1] On December 7, 2012, President Barack Obama signed Executive Order 13632 establishing the Hurricane Sandy Rebuilding Task Force for the purpose of ensuring government-wide and regional coordination and guidance as communities were making decisions about long-term rebuilding (see Hurricane Sandy Rebuilding Task Force, 2013a).

3. regional resilience
4. long-term efficacy and fiscal sustainability
5. environmentally sustainable and innovative solutions
6. targeted financial incentives
7. adherence to resilience performance standards.

Each principle is described at a general level in the task force report (see Hurricane Sandy Rebuilding Task Force, 2013a, pp. 49–53).

On behalf of the U.S. Department of Homeland Security and the Critical Infrastructure Security and Resilience Interagency Policy Committee's Subcommittee on Recovery and Mitigation, the RAND Corporation conducted an initial assessment of federal agencies' implementation of the guidelines. The main goal of this study was to identify the opportunities and challenges encountered when implementing the guidelines. Specific study objectives were as follows:

- Examine whether and how the guidelines have been implemented in decisions about how to spend federal funds to recover from Hurricane Sandy.
- Identify lessons learned from implementing the guidelines (including opportunities and challenges).
- Consider whether the same guidelines could be implemented when allocating federal funds for infrastructure in nonrecovery environments.

We conducted semistructured interviews from July 7 to September 19, 2014, with a total of 67 individuals employed by federal, state, and local government agencies and departments and nongovernmental organizations, some of which received Sandy supplemental funds for infrastructure projects. Interviewees were selected to reflect a diverse range of organization types, decisionmaker perspectives, and sectors. In some instances, interviewees provided documentation, such as announcements of federal funding opportunities or requests for proposals, that incorporated the resilience principles reflected in the guidelines as criteria for funding. An analysis of the interview notes and documents provided information on different approaches to implementing the guidelines, the opportunities or challenges encountered during implementation, and whether the guidelines would be feasible to implement in nonrecovery environments.

Our analysis indicated that the Infrastructure Resilience Guidelines reinforced the approach to resilience principles that many agencies have been pursuing in recent years. For example, several federal agencies had adopted the revised resilience principles for critical infrastructure developed by the American Society of Civil Engineers based on the lessons learned from Hurricane Katrina. Additionally, the President's *Climate Action Plan* (Executive Office of the President [EOP], 2013b) and Executive Orders 13653 (EOP, 2013c) and 13514 (EOP, 2009) encourage federal agencies to include resilience in policies, programs, and projects. Other relevant executive policy documents include Presidential Policy Directive 8 on National Preparedness (EOP, 2011); Presidential Policy Directive 21 on Critical Infrastructure Security and Resilience (EOP, 2013a); and the Department of Homeland Security's *National Infrastructure Protection Plan 2013: Partnering for Critical Infrastructure Security and Resilience* (DHS, 2013a). All of these efforts have been encouraging federal agencies to consider and incorporate resilience. As such, organizations already familiar with or embracing resilience principles found it easier to implement the guidelines than did those that were encountering these principles for the first time. Building community and infrastructure resilience via a *holistic systems approach* (i.e., one that underscores the dynamic links among human, social, physical, economic, and natural resources) was a new concept for some agencies and their grantees. For others, the focus on green infrastructure and nature-based solutions to deal with flooding and other storm impacts was a new pursuit. Our interviews also revealed that jurisdictions that had already established a good understanding of resilience and had identified data on communities and structures at risk were more efficient in putting the Sandy supplemental funds to work and prioritizing longer-term results over solving immediate needs.

The main challenges identified by interviewees underscored common difficulties in complex interagency initiatives. For instance, finding the right level of specificity in the guidelines is difficult if they are to be applied broadly yet meaningfully across diverse sectors and locations. Diverse contexts also result in diverse interpretations and metrics for resilience, which makes it difficult to know whether the guidelines are being followed or whether the intended progress is being made. Interviewees expressed a strong desire for a more streamlined approach to prioritizing the myriad guidance, executive orders, frameworks, and plans related to resilience. They also suggested that scientific evidence needs to be developed to guide decisions about how to meet resilience performance standards.

Overall, the guidelines were viewed as reflecting worthy resiliency principles that merit broader pursuit—and not just in a recovery context. In addition, the guidelines could be complemented with more in-depth consideration by the federal government about a comprehensive set of strategies for achieving resilience.

Acknowledgments

We gratefully acknowledge the support of interviewees from federal agencies and other organizations who provided thoughtful comments and insights in response to our questions about the Infrastructure Resilience Guidelines. We also acknowledge the support we received from members of the federal interagency Critical Infrastructure Security and Resilience Interagency Policy Committee's Subcommittee on Recovery and Mitigation, who provided important contextual information during the development of the interview protocol and verification of the plausibility of key themes during our analyses. Finally, we acknowledge Semira Ahdiyyih and Amy Grace Peele at RAND for their assistance with data collection, and Stephen Flynn and Lloyd Dixon for their editorial suggestions on an earlier draft of this report.

Abbreviations

CDBG	Community Development Block Grant
DHS	U.S. Department of Homeland Security
DOI	U.S. Department of the Interior
DOT	U.S. Department of Transportation
DRAA	Disaster Relief Appropriations Act
EOP	Executive Office of the President
EPA	U.S. Environmental Protection Agency
FEMA	Federal Emergency Management Agency
FHWA	Federal Highway Administration
FTA	Federal Transit Administration
HSDC	Homeland Security and Defense Center
HUD	U.S. Department of Housing and Urban Development
NFWF	National Fish and Wildlife Foundation
NIST	National Institute of Standards and Technology
NOAA	National Oceanic and Atmospheric Administration

NPPD	National Protection and Programs Directorate
RFP	request for proposals
USACE	U.S. Army Corps of Engineers

CHAPTER ONE

Introduction

The United States is increasingly threatened by natural disasters, reflecting the changing demographic and socioeconomic characteristics of coastal populations, the nation's aging infrastructure, and the influences of sea-level rise and other climate change effects (Munich Re, 2012; National Climatic Data Center, no date; Pielke et al., 2008). In October 2012, Hurricane Sandy struck the East Coast of the country, devastating communities across the region. Soon thereafter, the Disaster Relief Appropriations Act (DRAA) of February 29, 2013, or the Hurricane Sandy supplemental bill, provided more than $50 billion to help communities rebuild.

The scale of the Hurricane Sandy disaster motivated the federal government to examine how it might increase support for communities to be better prepared for existing and future threats, including those exacerbated by climate change. Recognizing the magnitude of the event and the rebuilding challenges faced by the region, President Barack Obama signed Executive Order 13632 on December 7, 2012, establishing the Hurricane Sandy Rebuilding Task Force to ensure governmentwide and regional coordination and guidance as communities make decisions about long-term rebuilding.

In the spring and summer of 2013, the Hurricane Sandy Rebuilding Task Force developed its Infrastructure Resilience Guidelines to ensure that federal agencies incorporated key principles of resilience into their formulation, evaluation, and prioritization of infrastructure investments related to Sandy rebuilding. The National Protection and Programs Directorate (NPPD) in the U.S. Department of Homeland

Security (DHS) co-led the working group responsible for developing the guidelines, which represent a shared understanding of the resilience principles that should be used by the federal agencies involved in rebuilding. Resilience involves enabling a region to withstand the effects of a disaster, respond effectively, recover quickly, adapt to changing conditions, and manage future disaster risk. The guidelines create a framework for evaluating investments in infrastructure during disaster recovery, whether through grants, loans, programs, or projects.

The aims of the guidelines are to (1) ensure that federal agencies have a consistent approach to building resilience and (2) improve decisionmaking to better protect communities and to ensure wise investment of scarce public resources by setting criteria for investment and by helping align projects with national policy goals. The seven principles in the guidelines are as follows:

1. comprehensive analysis—using comprehensive, forward-looking, and science-based analysis, including quantitative and qualitative measures of public health and safety, economic, social, environmental, and cascading impacts; changes to climate and developmental patterns; inherent risk and uncertainty; and the monetization of impacts
2. transparent and inclusive decision processes—applying multicriteria decision analysis, including a benefit-cost analysis and sharing decision criteria, evaluation processes, and findings with all stakeholders
3. regional resilience—working collaboratively with partners across all levels of governance and the private sector to promote a regional and cross-jurisdictional approach to resilience
4. long-term efficacy and fiscal sustainability—monitoring and evaluating the efficacy and sustainability of the implemented project, taking into account changing environmental conditions, such as sea-level rise or changing development patterns, using risk management tools and changing funding sources
5. environmentally sustainable and innovative solutions—ensuring that investments align with the President's *Climate Action Plan* and achieve operational resilience while also supporting federal

goals to promote innovation, sustainability, reduced environmental and public health impacts, and opportunities to leverage natural systems

6. targeted financial incentives—implementing meaningful financial incentives or funding requirements to promote the incorporation of resilience and risk mitigation into infrastructure projects
7. adherence to resilience performance standards—facilitating the development of resilience performance standards for infrastructure and using these performance standards when selecting infrastructure investments.

Each principle is described at a general level in the task force report (see Hurricane Sandy Rebuilding Task Force, 2013a, pp. 49–53). The task force recognized that the resilience principles reflected in the guidelines would be new to some agencies. Expectations about how agencies should incorporate the guidelines were described in a webinar (Hurricane Sandy Rebuilding Task Force, 2013b) and in follow-up communications. In general, the guidelines were incorporated into *Federal Register* notices or requests for proposals (RFPs) with selection criteria reflecting resilience principles. Most federal agencies—e.g., U.S. Department of Housing and Urban Development (HUD), Federal Emergency Management Agency (FEMA), U.S. Environmental Protection Agency (EPA), and U.S. Department of Transportation (DOT)—relied on existing programs to distribute the Sandy supplemental funds. An exception was the U.S. Department of the Interior (DOI), which developed a new program (examples are described in Chapter Two).

The guidelines were originally intended to be used for decisions related to the Sandy supplemental funds. However, the Hurricane Sandy Rebuilding Task Force (2013a) report recommended that the NPPD in DHS, under the policy leadership of the White House National Security Staff, establish an interagency process to assess the value and feasibility of expanding the use of the guidelines beyond Sandy recovery efforts. On behalf of DHS and the Critical Infrastructure Security and Resilience Interagency Policy Committee's Subcommittee on Recovery and Mitigation, the RAND Corporation conducted an initial assessment of federal agencies' implementation of the guidelines and opportunities or challenges to be considered regarding use of the guidelines when allocating federal funds for infrastructure in nonrecovery (i.e., nondisaster) contexts.

Goal and Objectives

The main goal of this study was to identify the opportunities and challenges encountered when implementing the Infrastructure Resilience Guidelines. Specific study objectives were as follows:

- Examine whether and how the guidelines have been implemented in decisions about how to spend federal funds to recover from Hurricane Sandy.
- Identify lessons learned from implementing the guidelines (including opportunities and challenges).
- Consider whether the same guidelines could be implemented when allocating federal funds for infrastructure in nonrecovery environments.

The Sandy supplemental funds were distributed primarily through HUD's Community Development Block Grant (CDBG) program, DOT's Emergency Relief Program, and FEMA's hazard mitigation and public assistance grants.[1] This initial assessment of the guidelines' implementation focused mainly on the processes related to funding allocation decisions (rather than on project activities per se). Such an

[1] HUD's CDBG program provides grants to state and local governments using a formula composed of several measures to address unique community development needs. DOT's Emergency Relief Program provides funds for emergency repairs of federal-aid highways, roads on federal lands, and public transportation systems that have suffered serious damage as a result of natural disasters or catastrophic failure from an external cause. FEMA provides grants to state and local governments after a major disaster declaration via the hazard mitigation program to implement long-term hazard mitigation measures and through the public assistance program for debris removal, emergency protective measures, and the repair, replacement, or restoration of disaster-damaged facilities.

examination was needed because many major infrastructure projects are just now getting started (two years after Hurricane Sandy) and they are, by definition, large and complicated projects that require lengthy planning, coordination, and approval processes. Thus, this study focused only on experiences during implementation of the guidelines and not on the effectiveness of the guidelines in increasing infrastructure resilience; we also focused only on infrastructure investments and not on noninfrastructure-related resilience.

Study Approach

To address the study's objectives, RAND researchers conducted 31 semistructured interviews with a total of 67 individuals from July 7 to September 19, 2014. The diverse sample included 48 individuals from 14 federal departments or agencies and 19 individuals from ten state and local governments and nongovernmental organizations, about 71 percent of which received Sandy supplemental funds for infrastructure projects (see Table 1.1 for interviewees' affiliations and roles). We included organizations that did not receive funds because, regardless of the Sandy supplemental, their missions and responsibilities indicated that they may have relevant perspectives on developing the guidelines, incorporating resilience parameters into allocation of federal funding, and building infrastructure resilience. Our goal was to solicit a diverse (as opposed to representative) set of views. Hence, we recruited interviewees using a purposive sampling technique to obtain a sample drawn from a range of organization types (e.g., federal, state, or local government; contractors; consultants; professional organizations; nongovernmental organizations), decisionmaker perspectives (e.g., agency director, project leader), and sectors (e.g., planning, urban development, security, health, environment, commerce, insurance, science standards, engineering, technology, transport).

During the interviews, we asked about how the guidelines had been used in different contexts, whether any opportunities or challenges were encountered during implementation, how the guidelines were communicated, and whether implementing the guidelines

Table 1.1
Interviewees' Affiliations and Roles

Category	Received Funding	Participated in Planning or Observed Process, but Did Not Receive Funding

Federal government	• DHS
	  ○ FEMA
	• DOI
	• DOT
	  ○ Federal Highway Administration (FHWA)
	  ○ Federal Transit Administration (FTA)
	• HUD
	• U.S. Army Corps of Engineers (USACE)
	• U.S. Department of Commerce
	  ○ National Oceanic and Atmospheric Administration (NOAA)
	• U.S. Department of Health and Human Services
	• U.S. Department of Veterans Affairs
	• U.S. Environmental Protection Agency
	• U.S. General Services Administration
	• U.S. Small Business Administration
		• Council on Environmental Quality
		• DHS
		  ○ Office of Policy
		• Office of Science and Technology Policy, White House
		• U.S. Department of Commerce
		  ○ Economic Development Administration
		  ○ National Institute of Standards and Technology (NIST)
		• U.S. Department of Treasury
		  ○ Federal Insurance Office

State and local government	• City of Norfolk, Virginia • City of Hoboken, New Jersey • New Jersey Governor's Office of Recovery and Rebuilding • New York City Mayor's Office • New York Rising Community Reconstruction Program	*Not relevant*
Contractors, consultants, professional organizations, and nongovernmental organizations	• American Littoral Society National Fish and Wildlife Foundation (NFWF)	• American Society of Civil Engineers • Insurance Institute for Business and Home Safety • The Infrastructure Security Partnership

NOTE: We also contacted individuals at several other federal agencies not listed here but did not interview them in detail because they did not receive funds for large infrastructure projects or did not participate significantly in planning or observing. (Examples include the U.S. Department of Energy, U.S. Department of Agriculture, U.S. Department of Defense, Office of the Under Secretary of Defense for Policy, Office of the Under Secretary of Defense for Homeland Defense, and U.S. Department of Health and Human Services Administration for Children and Families.)

would be feasible in nonrecovery environments (see Appendix A for the semistructured interview protocol). In some instances, interviewees provided documentation, such as announcements of federal funding opportunities or RFPs, that incorporated the resilience principles reflected in the guidelines as criteria for funding. We used a keywords-in-context technique (Tesch, 1990) to identify qualitative themes in interview notes and documents. The study methods are described in more detail in Appendix B.

Overview of This Report

In this report, we briefly summarize the assessment methods and results of the qualitative data analysis. Because early distribution of Sandy supplemental funding preceded the development of the guidelines, we present a timeline of related events to reflect that some events may have influenced implementation of the guidelines and some events may have been influenced by implementation of the guidelines. In Chapter Two, we describe what we heard in our interviews about how federal agencies have implemented the guidelines and how they communicated them to grantees who would carry out specific recovery projects. In Chapter Three, we identify lessons learned, including opportunities and challenges raised by implementing the guidelines. In Chapter Four, we share the opinions of our interviewees about whether and how implementation might be applied more broadly, not just in response to disasters. Finally, in Chapter Five, we present a summary of findings and conclusions from this study. The report will be useful for individuals and organizations contemplating how to improve infrastructure resilience on a national level. In particular, the findings will be informative for deliberations by members of federal interagency working groups, such as the Critical Infrastructure Security and Resilience Interagency Policy Committee's Subcommittee on Recovery and Mitigation.

CHAPTER TWO

How the Infrastructure Resilience Guidelines Have Been Implemented

To assess the perceived value and feasibility of the Infrastructure Resilience Guidelines (i.e., the extent to which the guidelines were considered worthwhile and were able to be implemented when distributing Sandy supplemental funds), we first needed to determine how the guidelines have been used in decisions about how to spend federal funds to recover from Hurricane Sandy. To address this question, we asked our interviewees to share their knowledge of the guidelines and how they have been implemented, if at all, in the context of their specific agency or jurisdiction's infrastructure investments. We explored both how implementation of the guidelines may change how federal funds for infrastructure are distributed and how the guidelines are communicated. Overall, we found that the two main factors influencing implementation relate to the timing of the release of the guidelines relative to the availability of Sandy supplemental funds and the mechanisms (approaches) available to implement them.

Timing of the Release of the Guidelines Relative to the Availability of Sandy Supplemental Funds

Table 2.1 shows a timeline of events, including Hurricane Sandy's landfall, funding availability and allocation, and the publication of the guidelines and other documents. Importantly, the guidelines were published after some of the Sandy supplemental funding had been distributed. For instance, HUD's CDBG funds are being distributed in three tranches (tranche 1 in March 2013, tranche 2 in November 2013,

Table 2.1
Timeline of Events Relevant to the Publication of the Infrastructure Resilience Guidelines

Date	Event
2009	American Society of Civil Engineers publishes *Guiding Principles for the Nation's Critical Infrastructure* (2009).
October 29, 2012	**Hurricane Sandy moves ashore near Brigantine, New Jersey.**
December 2012	NOAA and USACE collaborate on "Infrastructure Systems Rebuilding Principles" (released publicly on February 28, 2013; see NOAA and USACE, 2013).
January 29, 2013	President Obama signs the Disaster Relief Appropriations Act.
February 6, 2013	FTA publishes "Availability of Emergency Relief Funds in Response to Hurricane Sandy." (See FTA, 2013a.)
March 5, 2013	HUD publishes notice for "Allocations, Common Application, Waivers, and Alternative Requirements for Grantees Receiving Community Development Block Grant (CDBG) Disaster Recovery Funds in Response to Hurricane Sandy" (2013a, tranche 1).
March 11, 2013	USACE publishes *First Interim Report: Disaster Relief Appropriations Act, 2013* to provide the Senate and House Committees on Appropriations with an assessment of authorized construction projects and those under construction. (See USACE, 2013a.)
March 29, 2013	FTA publishes "Allocation of Public Transportation Emergency Relief Funds in Response to Hurricane Sandy." (See FTA, 2013b.)
April 2013	DOI receives its first of two allocations of Sandy supplemental funding (directed to bureaus to, for instance, repair the Statue of Liberty, Gateway, Ellis Island, and an oil test facility; see DOI, 2013).
April 19, 2013	HUD publishes notice for "Clarifying Guidance, Waivers, and Alternative Requirements for Hurricane Sandy Grantees in Receipt of Community Development Block Grant Disaster Recovery Funds" (2013b). The notice clarifies the general requirements and changes the elevation requirements from the March 5, 2013, notice.
May 1, 2013	EPA releases a memo regarding DRAA 2013 funding to provide guidance on requirements for state revolving Capital Fund grants. (See Sawyers and Grevatt, 2013.)
May 29, 2013	FTA publishes notice of "Second Allocation of Public Transportation Emergency Relief Funds in Response to Sandy: Response, Recovery, and Resiliency." (See FTA, 2013c.) HUD publishes notice of "Allocations, Waivers, and Alternative Requirements for Grantees Receiving Community Development Block Grant Disaster Recovery Funds in Response to Disasters Occurring in 2011 or 2012." (See HUD, 2013c.)

Table 2.1—Continued

Date	Event
May 30, 2013	USACE publishes *Second Interim Report Disaster Relief Appropriations Act, 2013* to provide the Senate and House Committees on Appropriations with assessments of previously authorized but unconstructed projects and projects under study by the Corps for reducing flooding and storm damage risks in the affected area.
June 2013	DOI's Strategic Sciences Group develops resilience criteria to evaluate potential projects for internal competition for Sandy supplemental funds.
June 18, 2013	FEMA publishes Mitigation Policy FP-108-024-01 (FEMA, 2013) to identify and quantify the types of environmental benefits it will consider in its benefit-cost analysis for acquisition projects under Hazard Mitigation Assistance programs. Traditionally, FEMA considers the cost of the mitigation project and the cost associated with future damages avoided in determining cost effectiveness.
June 25, 2013	President Obama's *Climate Action Plan* is released. (See Executive Office of the President [EOP], 2013b.)
July 19, 2013	USACE promulgates guidance requiring that the Comprehensive Study due to Congress in January 2015 include a multiagency framework for identifying and reducing coastal flood risks, including those posed by sea-level rise and climate change (inclusive of recommendations for modification of existing risk reduction projects where appropriate).
August 2013	**The Hurricane Sandy Rebuilding Task Force (2013a) releases *Hurricane Sandy Rebuilding Strategy: Stronger Communities, a Resilient Region* (see pp. 49–53 for the Infrastructure Resilience Guidelines).**
August 28, 2013	NOAA posts a federal funding opportunity for 2013 DRAA funding for coastal resilience networks. (See NOAA, 2013.)
August 2013	DOI announces that NFWF will administer the Hurricane Sandy Coastal Resiliency Competitive Grant. (See NFWF, 2013.)
October 28, 2013	DOI's second of two allocations of Sandy supplemental funding is released via an external RFP, the Hurricane Sandy Coastal Resiliency Competitive Grants Program.
November 1, 2013	The President issues Executive Order 13653, "Preparing the United States for the Impacts of Climate Change." It instructs federal agencies to consider climate change in their policies and procedures. (See EOP, 2013c.)

Table 2.1—Continued

Date	Event
November 6, 2013	USACE publishes *Hurricane Sandy Coastal Projects Performance Evaluation Study: Disaster Relief Appropriations Act, 2013* (USACE, 2013c), which reports findings from an evaluation of 75 completed coastal storm damage reduction projects in the North Atlantic Division (as well as 31 projects in the Great Lakes and Ohio River Division and nine projects in the South Atlantic Division) and includes preliminary discussion of observed impediments to delivery of more-comprehensive risk reduction along coastlines affected by Hurricane Sandy.
November 18, 2013	HUD publishes "Notice for Second Allocation, Waivers, and Alternative Requirements for Grantees Receiving Community Development Block Grant (CDBG) Disaster Recovery Funds in Response to Hurricane Sandy" (tranche 2; see HUD, 2013d). The Infrastructure Resilience Guidelines are incorporated in the Notice.
December 23, 2013	FEMA publishes guidance allowing Hazard Mitigation Assistance applicants to incorporate sea-level rise in their Hazard Mitigation Grant Program and Public Assistance Grant Program projects, where it is cost-effective to do so. (See Wright, 2013.)
December 26, 2013	FTA publishes "Notice of Funding Availability for Resilience Projects in Response to Hurricane Sandy" for tranche 3 of funding (FTA, 2013d). Awards were expected to be announced in late 2014.
January 31, 2014	NFWF requires proposals to integrate resilience guidelines. (See NFWF, 2014.)
April 21, 2014	FEMA publishes Mitigation Policy 203-074-1 (FEMA, 2014), requiring recipients of Hazard Mitigation Grant funding to meet the standards of American Society of Civil Engineers standard 24, Flood Resistant Design and Construction, a consensus set of flood design and construction standards developed under the auspices of the American Society of Civil Engineers and incorporated in the current edition of the International Residential Code.
June 3, 2014	HUD publishes "Notice of Second Allocation, Waivers, and Alternative Requirements for Grantees Receiving Community Development Block Grant (CDBG) Disaster Recovery Funds in Response to Disasters Occurring in 2013." (See HUD, 2014.)
September 30, 2014	EPA to make awards to subrecipients.
Late 2014	Tranche 3 of HUD Sandy supplemental funds to be allocated.
January 2015	USACE North Atlantic Coast Comprehensive Study due to Congress.

and tranche 3 expected in late 2014). The guidelines were published between the first two tranches, in mid-August 2013. Consequently, decisions related to tranche 2 were influenced by the guidelines to varying degrees, but early spending decisions related to tranche 1 funds were not influenced by the guidelines. Nonetheless, Sandy funding issued prior to the release of the guidelines may still have been aligned with similar resilience principles because of preexisting initiatives that already guided decisionmakers (e.g., the collaboration between NOAA and USACE on Infrastructure Systems Rebuilding Principles [NOAA and USACE, 2013]; the resilience criteria developed by DOI's Strategic Sciences Group).[1]

Publishing the guidelines after some of the Sandy supplemental funding was distributed was problematic for some organizations. In some instances, interviewees noted that design specifications for projects initiated prior to the guidelines' release needed to be reviewed or revised to meet the guidelines (e.g., accounting for changing environmental conditions, such as sea-level rise). In other instances, the project design or process did not need to be altered, but additional explanation was needed from grantees to explain how the project met the guidelines.

Mechanisms for Implementing the Guidelines

In general, the guidelines have been incorporated into *Federal Register* notices or RFPs (covering many different possible projects, with selection criteria reflecting principles in the guidelines), with follow-up communications and ongoing monitoring to refine project designs. Most federal agencies (e.g., HUD, FEMA, EPA, DOT) have relied on existing programs to distribute the Sandy supplemental funds. An exception was DOI, which developed a new program. (See Table 2.2 for sample programs.) Each program has required qualitatively different mechanisms (approaches) to implement the guidelines. Although we cannot compare practices of agencies that were and were not instructed

---

[1] Some interviewees also noted that the draft guidelines were circulated to agencies as early as May 2013, though not formally issued until the task force report was finalized.

Table 2.2
Sample Programs Used to Distribute Sandy Supplemental Funds

Agency	Program
HUD	Community Development Block Grant—Disaster Recovery
DHS FEMA	Hazard Mitigation Grant Program; Public Assistance Grant Program
DOT	Public Transportation Emergency Relief Program
EPA	State Revolving Fund
DOI	New program including an internal competition for bureaus and an external competition for local communities. The program was administered by NFWF.

to implement the guidelines (because the task force recommended that the guidelines apply to all agencies), it seems that the guidelines did contribute to the modification of existing programs or development of the new program for distributing Sandy supplemental funds.

HUD Adapted an Existing Program

HUD used the existing CDBG program to distribute Sandy supplemental funds.2 The Infrastructure Resilience Guidelines were fully incorporated into the requirements for HUD's tranche 2 CDBG disaster recovery funds for major infrastructure projects (defined as *covered projects*; HUD, 2013d). These projects have a total cost of $50 million or more, including at least $10 million in CDBG disaster recovery funds. The notice was further informed by Rebuild by Design, an initiative of the Hurricane Sandy Rebuilding Task Force and HUD. Because the CDBG program was created for community development rather than disaster recovery, HUD needed to amend, waive, and revise the requirements to apply the CDBG program to a recovery context (see HUD, 2013a, 2013b).

To ensure that grantees (in this case, affected states and New York City) incorporate the guidelines, HUD requires the grantees to develop plans to address each of the seven principles (HUD, 2013d).

[2] Kousky and Shabman (2013, p. 5) note that Congress began using the CDBG mechanism for distributing disaster relief funds after Hurricane Katrina.

HUD also relies on the Sandy Regional Infrastructure Resilience Coordination Group (co-led by HUD and FEMA), a forum through which grantees, HUD, and approximately 11 other federal agencies vet and evaluate the extent to which CDBG proposals address the guidelines, at least for covered projects. Notably, HUD's influence on the prioritization of projects is somewhat limited once the funds are distributed because the states are responsible for identifying and selecting priority projects.

In April and May 2013, initial action plans were developed by New York City, New York State, and New Jersey, outlining their plans for the CDBG funding. Because the guidelines were published subsequent to those plans, these jurisdictions needed to amend their original action plans to address the guidance. HUD has committed to on-site monitoring of the grantees twice a year, obtaining documented evidence to gauge both compliance and grantees' understanding of requirements. Once grantees start implementing the plans, they will submit quarterly performance reports. HUD also communicates weekly with grantees on a variety of topics (see Appendix C for examples of sample grantees).

FEMA Used an Existing Program

Another example of an agency using an existing program is FEMA, which used its Hazard Mitigation Grant Program and Public Assistance Grant Program, which already had in place processes consistent with the guidelines. Authorized under Section 404 of the Robert T. Stafford Disaster Relief and Emergency Assistance Act, the Hazard Mitigation Grant Program provides grants to state and local governments after a major disaster declaration to implement long-term hazard mitigation measures. The purpose of the program is to reduce the loss of life and property due to natural disasters and to enable immediate implementation of mitigation measures following recovery from a disaster. The Public Assistance Grant Program is more focused on providing assistance so that communities can quickly respond to and recover from major disasters. Eligible activities include debris removal, emergency protective measures, and the repair, replacement, or restoration of disaster-damaged, publicly owned facilities and the facilities of certain private nonprofit organizations. The program also encourages protecting damaged facilities from future events during the recovery process by providing assistance with hazard mitigation measures.

One modification to FEMA's existing process came from Section 428 of the 2013 Sandy Recovery Improvement Act. This section allowed recovery projects to be paid based on estimates, which sped up recovery. FEMA also elevated focus on resilience concepts by issuing memos with guidance to include sea-level rise data (December 23, 2013) and environmental benefits (June 18, 2013) into benefit-cost analyses.

DOT Used an Existing Program

DOT is an agency with a long history of responding to emergencies and therefore has existing emergency rule authority granted by Congress and established processes through which emergency relief funding is distributed (such as the emergency relief programs of FTA and FHWA). Following Hurricane Sandy, DOT was able to distribute funds for immediate response and recovery needs, set aside funds for future recovery needs, and distribute funds for major long-term resilience projects, including through a competitive process. Resilience principles are evident in the FTA's competitive resilience notice of funding availability and allocations from December 26, 2013 (tranche 3 of its Sandy supplemental funds), which was developed around the same time as the guidelines. The notice explicitly states that FTA considered the Infrastructure Resilience Guidelines in developing its solicitation, and the evaluation criteria reflect these principles. This approach builds on resilience principles (e.g., regional collaboration) already covered in the existing transportation planning process.

EPA Used an Existing Program

A third example of an agency using an existing program is the EPA's Office of Water, which was instructed by the DRAA to use the existing State Revolving Fund process for any municipal water systems seeking assistance. Interviewees noted that existing procedures captured many of the principles in the guidelines. The states, under the established Revolving Fund process, identified projects and accepted multiple applications from affected communities. From those applications, the states selected projects for which intended use plans are still being developed. Intended use plans are required from states as part of the process to request federal capitalization grants, which describes the intended use of all State Revolving Funds expected to be available and will be matched with 20 percent from state funds. Although the existing Revolving Fund process primarily drove funding decisions, the EPA did incorporate resilience principles such as socioecological interdependencies in ways not considered before. For instance, guidance provided in a memo from the Office of Wastewater Management (4201M) and the Office of Ground Water and Drinking Water (4601M) explained that projects eligible under the DRAA include planning projects that analyze the best approach to integrate system and community sustainability and resiliency priorities.

DOI Established a New Program

In contrast to the above existing programs used to distribute Sandy supplemental funds, DOI established a new, one-time program to distribute funds in two ways: through an internal competition for bureaus (awarded in October 2013) and an external competition for local communities (awarded in June 2014). This new program was developed through a partnership with NFWF, which was contracted to administer the award program according to criteria established by DOI. In the following sections, we describe briefly how the guidelines were followed as the money flowed downstream from the Sandy supplemental program to agencies and grantees carrying out specific resilience projects.

Internal Competition

For the internal competition, DOI asked its bureaus to submit projects related to DOI assets, refuges, park service units, tribes, and scientific advancement that would build resilience to future storms in the Sandy-affected area. The focus was on green infrastructure,[3] improving community resilience, nature-based solutions, and research on how to

---

[3] The NFWF RFP defines green infrastructure as follows: "These projects may include rebuilding natural systems in communities, such as wetlands, floodplains and forests, or applying green/'nature-based' stormwater management techniques including projects that

incorporate nature-based solutions. Because the internal competition was on a faster track than the external competition, DOI asked its Strategic Sciences Group to help it establish resilience criteria against which it could evaluate the merits of potential projects.[4] These criteria were developed at about the same time as the guidelines and reflected similar principles. DOI communicated these resilience criteria to its bureaus by having the scientists who developed the criteria also explain them. The criteria were also expressed in the guidance that served as the internal RFP for the bureaus to request funding for resilience projects. Proposals needed to explain how the project would meet the resilience criteria, and all proposals were reviewed by an interagency team of technical experts.

External Competition

The purpose of the external competition was to provide grant funding for resilience efforts to state and local governments, as well as nonprofit and academic institutions. Like the internal competition, the focus was on green infrastructure, improving community resilience, and nature-based solutions. In developing the grant competition and the criteria that would be used to evaluate the projects, NFWF worked with staff from DOI headquarters and a regional leadership team that included representatives from all of the bureaus. In developing the grant criteria, NFWF took into account the resilience criteria developed by the Strategic Sciences Group and the Infrastructure Resilience Guidelines. NFWF further complemented those criteria with its Coastal Resilience Conservation Framework. The framework took the effort a step further by attempting to define outcomes related to the program. It incorporated the resilience criteria of DOI's Strategic Sciences Group and the larger set of recommendations developed by federal agencies, including the Infrastructure Resilience Guidelines, and developed an investment strategy to help accomplish DOI's goals.

---

infiltrate, capture and reuse stormwater to maintain or restore natural hydrology and prevent overflows and flooding" (NFWF, 2014).

[4] The Strategic Sciences Group was established after the Deepwater Horizon Oil Spill in the Gulf of Mexico to assess immediate science needs following a disaster. This group is composed of scientists from the U.S. Geological Survey and the National Park Service.

NFWF's board would now like to see the resiliency principles applied to all its work to the extent feasible (some examples of DOI grantees via NFWF can be found in Appendix C).

Summary of Timing and Mechanisms for Implementing the Guidelines

The two main factors influencing implementation of the Infrastructure Resilience Guidelines relate to the timing of the release of the guidelines relative to the availability of Sandy supplemental funds and the mechanisms available to implement the guidelines. Importantly, the guidelines were published after some of the Sandy supplemental funding had already been distributed. As a result, design specifications for some projects initiated prior to the guidelines' release needed to be reviewed or revised to meet the guidelines (e.g., to account for sea-level rise projections). In general, the guidelines have been incorporated into *Federal Register* notices and RFPs, with follow-up communications and ongoing monitoring to refine project designs. Most federal agencies (e.g., HUD, FEMA, DOT, EPA) have relied on existing programs to distribute the Sandy supplemental funds. The nature of the guidelines meant that modifications to some existing programs were needed (e.g., via waivers for HUD's CDBG Disaster Recovery program). In other cases (e.g., EPA), the DRAA directed the agency to use an existing process. In contrast, DOI developed a new program to address the guidelines. Criteria for funding decisions in DOI's new program took into account the resilience criteria developed by its Strategic Sciences Group, the guidelines, and the NFWF Coastal Resilience Conservation Framework. These criteria required applicants to describe how proposed projects would promote resilience, green infrastructure, and regional collaboration.

CHAPTER THREE

Lessons Learned from Implementing the Infrastructure Resilience Guidelines

The Infrastructure Resilience Guidelines reflect an innovative approach to encouraging federal agencies to incorporate resilience principles in their infrastructure investment decisions. To identify how the guidelines might be useful for guiding future decisions by federal agencies, we explored the opportunities and challenges encountered in their current implementation. Evaluating lessons learned contributes to the iterative refinement of best practices for complex resilience programs by providing information about the content of the guidelines, processes related to implementing the guidelines, and conditions under which the guidelines are implemented that facilitate or impede progress toward national resilience. To identify lessons learned, we asked our interviewees to describe how implementation was facilitated, what challenges were encountered, and what, if any, modifications they would suggest to improve the guidelines. Below, we report examples of suggestions that surfaced as repeated themes in the interviews and illustrated diverse perspectives.

Lessons Learned from Conditions That Facilitated Implementation of the Guidelines

In the following sections, we describe how implementation of the guidelines was facilitated when federal agencies and other organizations were already familiar with or using similar resilience principles in their decisionmaking, when there was broad federal government focus on resilience concepts, and when there was an established community vision and planning process for resilience.

Agencies Incorporate Resilience Principles into Standard Processes

Prior to Hurricane Sandy, most of the federal agencies represented by our interviews reported that they already had a good understanding of key resilience principles and had initiated efforts to incorporate the principles into their standard processes. For instance, many interviewees reported that they had considered the concept of rebuilding structures and systems to more-resilient standards to better withstand future storms. Consensus among agencies about key resilience principles reflected that several related efforts occurred around the same time that the guidelines were developed, which led to considerable cross-pollination—for instance, between the DOI Strategic Sciences Group that was developing resilience criteria (finalized in June 2013) to govern DOI allocation decisions and the Sandy task force in its development of the guidelines (released in August 2013). Similarly, NOAA and USACE began developing joint rebuilding principles several months before the task force began its efforts, publicly releasing a report in 2013. The NOAA-USACE collaboration incorporated a set of principles by the American Society of Civil Engineers (from 2009), developed in response to lessons learned from Hurricane Katrina. Although there is not a one-to-one correspondence, the seven principles listed in the task force's guidelines overlap significantly with the principles outlined by the NOAA-USACE collaboration and the principles in the American Society of Civil Engineers' guide to protecting public safety, health, and welfare (see Table 3.1).

Unsurprisingly, organizations already embracing resilience principles found it easier to implement the Infrastructure Resilience Guidelines (e.g., DOI, DOT, FEMA, NIST, NOAA, USACE, U.S. Economic Development Administration, and U.S. General Services Administration). For instance, FHWA has historically used the term *betterment* rather than *resiliency*, which applies as long as improvements meet the requirements of a risk-based benefit-cost analysis. Due to this historical focus, DOT already had a culture of resilience, and its emergency response program has been around for 80 years. Additionally,

Table 3.1
Resilience Principles Presented by the Hurricane Sandy Rebuilding Task Force, the NOAA-USACE Collaboration, and the American Society of Civil Engineers

Hurricane Sandy Rebuilding Task Force Infrastructure Resilience Guidelines (2013)	NOAA-USACE Infrastructure Systems Rebuilding Principles (2013)	American Society of Civil Engineers Guiding Principles for the Nation's Critical Infrastructure (2009)
• Comprehensive analysis. • Transparent and inclusive decision processes.	• Promote increased recognition and awareness of risks and consequences. • Collaborate across multiple government and nongovernment entities to develop long-term strategies.	• Quantify, communicate, and manage risk.
• Regional resilience.	• Pursue a systems approach that incorporates natural, social, and built systems as a whole.	• Employ an integrated systems approach.
• Long-term efficacy and fiscal sustainability. • Environmentally sustainable and innovative solutions. • Adherence to resilience performance standards. • Targeted financial incentives.	• Develop long-term strategies. • Identify and pursue economically viable solutions. • Promote the integration of natural and built systems.	• Exercise sound leadership, management, and stewardship in decision-making processes. • Adapt critical infrastructure in response to dynamic conditions and practices.

climate adaptation projects have been going on for almost a decade on the nonrecovery side because DOT recognized that climate change is an important issue to consider during project planning and design (see DOT, 2013). As a second example, the FTA broadly incorporates similar principles in its metropolitan and statewide transportation planning process—a highly developed process that involves all regional partners.

Similarly, a third example is the U.S. Economic Development Administration's experience incorporating resilience parameters into grant funding. For more than a decade, it has used the term *resilience* as a factor tracked in projects. In this way, it has focused on building flexibility at the project level (rather than at the benefit-cost analysis level) so that staff and applicants consider how resilience plays a role in the full context of the project.

Notably, the resilience principle that seemed to be the newest for agencies was the focus on building resilience via a *holistic systems approach* (i.e., one that underscores the dynamic links among human, social, physical, economic, and natural resources). This principle prompted some agencies (e.g., NOAA) to focus more on integrating the built environment and natural systems and other agencies (e.g., HUD) to focus more than before on green infrastructure. In contrast, NIST has historically focused on systems-level thinking when establishing the technical basis for performance-based standards for building design (for earthquake hazard reduction, structural fire resistance, and collapse prevention, for example). NIST has been building on that work by exploring how a resilient-built environment supports community social systems and, in 2015, expects to release its Disaster Resilience Framework that supports the development of model resilience guidelines. Consistent with the principles in the task force guidelines, the NIST approach to resilience includes considering interconnected systems, cascading effects, a regional perspective, delineation of performance requirements, and flexibility to implement innovative solutions to meet performance goals (rather than prescribing solutions).

Broad Federal Government Focus on Resilience Principles

Interviewees reported that implementation of the guidelines was facilitated by a broad federal government focus on resilience principles via multiple initiatives. Introducing the guidelines in the context of broad federal focus on the value of building resilience meant that the guidelines were viewed as providing additional support for agency efforts, rather than sending them in different directions. Naturally, a common focus across federal agencies supports alignment of public investment decision processes with national policy goals.

For instance, the guidelines are aligned with President Obama's *Climate Action Plan* (EOP, 2013b, released June 25, 2013, ahead of the guidelines) and Executive Orders 13653 (EOP, 2013c, released November 1, 2013) and 13514 (EOP, 2009, released October 5, 2009), which led the Council on Environmental Quality to challenge agencies to include resilience to climate change in their policies, programs, projects, and operations as they develop their individual adaptation plans. Additional executive policy documents that highlight the importance of resilience include Presidential Policy Directive 8 on National Preparedness (EOP, 2011), Presidential Policy Directive 21 on Critical Infrastructure Security and Resilience (EOP, 2013a), and DHS's *National Infrastructure Protection Plan 2013: Partnering for Critical Infrastructure Security and Resilience* (DHS, 2013a). The guidelines are also aligned with FEMA's 2013 National Mitigation Framework (DHS, 2013b, updated in May 2014) and 2011 National Disaster Recovery Framework.

Given that many federal agencies had already established a resilience focus, implementing the guidelines did not require them to develop new policies or procedures. However, some interviewees did report sharpening their focus on specific resilience concepts. For instance, on December 23, 2013, FEMA issued guidance to incorporate sea-level rise into hazard mitigation assistance benefit-cost analysis. This guidance explained that FEMA is making the sea-level rise information available and providing tools for benefit-cost analyses to integrate climate change considerations into grant investment strategies. Rather than calculating benefits on existing conditions and past hazard events, this memo allows communities to use modeling data for future risks. Thus, FEMA was able to provide additional support for a forward-looking approach, consistent with the comprehensive analysis principle in the guidelines, and consistent with the broader federal focus on building long-term resilience.

In addition, some interviewees noted that the broad focus on resilience across agencies has catalyzed communities outside of federal agencies to adopt a resilience lens. One positive consequence of adopting a systems approach, for instance, is that it can help a project gain momentum with a wider variety of stakeholders and potentially attract longer-term support for infrastructure projects. The potential for agreement on robust strategies for building long-term resilience is likely greater when there is a broader understanding across stakeholders about the need for a multifaceted approach in a dynamic coastal area that serves a range of socioeconomic functions and provides various ecosystem benefits. Agencies emphasized the importance of including the guidelines in grant guidance and providing a needed incentive for grantees to implement these ideas in a consistent way.

Established Community Vision and Planning Processes Prior to Disaster

Many interviewees emphasized the importance of establishing a community vision (and aligning projects, to the extent possible) prior to a disaster so that communities can aim for that vision postdisaster and ensure that the vision is not overlooked because of immediate needs and stress. Interviewees observed that various states and localities had very different starting points in terms of their level of preparedness, both in their understanding of the resilience principles reflected in the guidelines and in any planning to that effect prior to Hurricane Sandy. They further observed that a jurisdiction's level of preparedness influenced its ability to put the Sandy supplemental funds to work in an organized and efficient manner that focused on predetermined longer-term goals for its community. To illustrate, although the final NYC Special Initiative for Rebuilding and Resiliency report was published after Hurricane Sandy, in June 2013, the planning process had started two years prior (City of New York, 2013). The substantial planning and modeling that had already occurred accelerated the rate at which infrastructure resilience projects could be identified, prioritized, and implemented in New York City. Similarly, the City of Norfolk, Virginia, had been thinking about resiliency since approximately 2008, particularly with respect to coastal flooding. Norfolk was one of the cities selected by the Rockefeller Foundation's 100 Resilient Cities initiative and now has a chief resilience officer. As a result, officials there had a good understanding of the issue and data on communities and structures at risk. The resilience principles challenged them to build on their existing data and knowledge, which allowed a more efficient and resilience-responsive approach.

Lessons Learned from Challenges Posed by the Guidelines

In the following sections, we describe some of the challenges that have been encountered during implementation of the Infrastructure Resilience Guidelines, along with interviewees' thoughts on how these challenges could be addressed. From these challenges and the interviewees' suggestions, we can identify lessons learned for both improving the guidelines and taking other actions that would facilitate their implementation in the future. These lessons relate to balancing generality versus specificity in the guidelines, clarifying and aligning the meanings and metrics of resilience, finding sufficient resources, simplifying overlapping and competing requirements, and developing the science about what increases resilience effectively.

Balance Generality Versus Specificity

The main challenge we heard from interviewees related to finding the right balance between making the guidelines broad enough to apply to all agencies and contexts, but not so broad as to call into question what actions count in meeting each principle. Interviewees acknowledged that the guidelines needed to be worded broadly to achieve interagency consensus and be applicable across different agency responsibilities, but also worded in a way that provided enough detail on the methods and outcomes that would be compatible with resilience principles. Interviewees generally thought that flexibility and an emphasis on innovation would enable agencies to make the guidelines relevant to their missions and provide the latitude needed to work within existing processes or regulations. At the same time, many interviewees suggested that it would be helpful to have an additional level of definition (and concrete metrics or benchmarks) in the guidelines to help determine what is intended, how to prioritize and implement the guidelines, and how to determine whether they are meeting requirements.

For instance, compared with other principles, interviewees noted that *comprehensive analysis* is described in more detail and was less confusing. Nonetheless, interviewees still raised questions about the degree to which each of the factors (e.g., environmental, economic, social, health) needed to be considered in a comprehensive analysis. The principle *regional resilience* seemed to be slightly more confusing than other principles, with interviewees expressing uncertainty about whether it is adequate simply to let other agencies know that an activity is under way or whether other agencies should have a formal place on the planning team. Interviewees asked for more information on the intended and specific outcome of regional resilience.

Perhaps most confusing for interviewees was the principle of *resilience performance standards.* Interviewees suggested that it would be helpful to have specific examples of the types of work that would meet such standards. For instance, grantees might already be familiar with technical variables typically found in building codes, but less familiar with other organizational, social, economic, or system variables that may also be examined against a standard. Illustrations of the best measures and methods to capture process improvements, business continuity, and other nonphysical means would help to clarify expectations of the federal government. One valuable outcome of considering specific examples in depth is that additional tools may be identified—for instance, to help decisionmakers balance difficult trade-offs. This would support answers to the following types of policy questions:

- How should decisionmakers balance environmental concerns and preferences for risk reduction in a specific setting?
- What methods should be followed when different stakeholder perspectives affect one another in a systems context?

One community may want risk-reduction measures that rely on hardening, such as building sea walls, while another may be looking for nature-based solutions that support ecological functions and habitats along the coastline. When the two approaches are implemented adjacently, this may compromise the performance of both and deliver a less-reliable solution for the entire region. Providing sources for technical assistance, tools, or data in interpreting and implementing the principles in the guidelines would be helpful for both agencies and grantees.

Clarify and Align Resilience Meanings and Metrics

A second challenge encountered when implementing the guidelines is that many resilience meanings and metrics seem to be used by various stakeholders, which can cause confusion about goals and methods for building resilience. Interviewees reported diverse interpretations of *resilience*, including readiness, preparedness, system resilience, economic resilience, speed of recovery, recovery to address a current need, recovery to a desired future state, and mitigation. Similarly, it is important to clarify at what scale we are talking about resilience because it will likely mean different benefits, costs, and other outcomes for a business, community, city, county, state, or regional entity. Consequently, there are also many different metrics that might be used to measure resilience, depending on the meaning adopted. Recognizing that resilience means different things in different contexts, the challenge is to acknowledge that diverse definitions exist and, consequently, that diverse methods and metrics exist. Interviewees underscored the need to be explicit and transparent about what is intended in a given context to increase communication and understanding. Examples of methods and metrics will be most helpful when they are presented with a broader explanation of the rationale and motivations underlying resilience principles.

Find Ways to Access Appropriate and Sufficient Resources and Expertise

Implementing some of the principles (e.g., conducting a comprehensive analysis) might be beyond the expertise of some community development staff at the state or city level. Staff trained as grant managers do not necessarily have the technical skills needed to address the more substantive issues contained in the guidelines. Some grantees needed help understanding that, in fact, there may be existing studies to draw from that could be used for the comprehensive analysis and that new analyses were not necessarily needed. However, the challenges inherent in locating and integrating diverse data still need to be addressed.

Although different types of variables from different sources are increasingly available for systems-level analyses, accurate implementation of such an approach requires specialized knowledge and training and additional resources such as staff time and computing facilities. Regional collaboration on system-wide planning also becomes increasingly time consuming as larger numbers of stakeholders are consulted and views and values are reconciled. In addition, HUD's November 18, 2013, *Federal Register* notice required a much greater level of federal scrutiny over specific infrastructure investments not only from HUD and the Regional Coordination Working Group but also from all partner agencies (e.g., USACE, DOT, EPA). This was a new role for many agencies, requiring a heavier reliance on colleagues (such as meteorologists at NOAA and engineers at USACE) to provide or interpret technical information in their project review processes. Some interviewees suggested that improving interagency communication at the federal level would help improve access to and use of available information and technical capacities.

Streamline and Integrate Overlapping or Competing Requirements or Needs

While the consistent message regarding resilience across initiatives and various levels of government was viewed as a positive development, both agencies and grantees expressed a desire for reduced complexity and redundancy. Apart from regulatory requirements and agency mission, which take primacy, there is little guidance on how to prioritize the guidelines relative to other initiatives or whether they in fact differ substantively. For grantees, each pot of federal funding for which they apply comes with a different set of criteria that reflect similar but distinct guidance. Some interviewees noted that attending to multiple sets of guidance has shifted resources toward coordinating among the various requirements in the allocation and planning processes, rather than toward the infrastructure itself. Ensuring that the intent of the sets of guidance are understood and addressed adequately—and that action to address one set of guidance does not contradict another—takes dedicated resources. However, because infrastructure projects have a longer time horizon, some interviewees speculated that the cost of those additional resources might be low.

Develop the Science

Although the guidelines present principles that are consistent with state-of-the-art thinking about achieving resilience, additional work is needed to clarify specific standards most likely to improve resilience. In particular, some interviewees noted that complying with the principle of adhering to *resilience performance standards* was challenging, at least in part, because of a lack of scientific evidence to guide decisions about what standards have been proven effective and thus what specifications are needed. In the context of its Disaster Resilience Framework, NIST is attempting to develop the science behind the guidelines so that jurisdictions and individuals charged with implementing resilience standards will have some assurance that they will have a positive effect. Evidence-based approaches to building resilience will help stakeholders to make informed decisions about infrastructure investments that are in line with best practices. More specifically, if new science suggests that a building code needs to be revised, then this sends a community and market signal about what practices will ensure that infrastructure can withstand future conditions. In addition, some interviewees proposed that it would be worth examining whether and how the increased federal interagency partnership during the Sandy recovery process has resulted in better or more-inclusive decisionmaking and whether and how that may be related to increased infrastructure resilience in the long term. Ideally, a third party would be used to assess and validate metrics and determine whether projects actually followed the recommended standards and ultimately contributed to resilience. Some agencies (e.g., DOI) have a plan to conduct such an evaluation.

Another way that science is developing is by expanding methods for capturing ecosystem benefits, which are often hard to value and may not be factored into benefit-cost equations. Similarly, other indirect benefits to society from resiliency initiatives may be hard to quantify, evaluate, and incorporate into analyses, but robust methods are critical so that effective programs and processes can be identified and repeated. Recent efforts have attempted to quantify various costs and benefits from socioeconomic factors or national beneficial functions of infrastructure. These factors reflect dynamic conditions and a changing environment, and we need to determine the most-robust methods for incorporating them into benefit-cost analyses so that the most-broadly effective approaches to building resilience can be implemented nationwide.

Summary of Lessons Learned from Implementation of the Guidelines

Based on feedback from interviewees, we identified several lessons learned, including both opportunities and challenges encountered with the current implementation of the Infrastructure Resilience Guidelines. The lessons are summarized in Table 3.2. As would be expected, implementation of the guidelines is facilitated when similar resilience principles are already being used by agencies and organizations in their decisions about resource distribution. In addition, the broad focus on resilience principles across various federal-level initiatives has provided an organizational framework that creates a general emphasis on—and increases awareness of—how to build infrastructure resilience in innovative and more-effective ways. Furthermore, entities with preexisting efforts to conceptualize and analyze community needs (i.e., before a disaster) tend to be more efficient in implementing the guidelines. The main challenges identified by interviewees underscored common difficulties in complex interagency initiatives, leading to several lessons learned for improving the guidelines and setting the conditions for effective guideline implementation.

In addition to the lessons learned in Table 3.2, we have proposed potential types of stakeholders (actors) that may have a primary role in addressing each lesson, based on discussions with interviewees and the authors' observations of the opportunities and responsibilities various stakeholders described being afforded them. Identifying primary actors will help highlight strategies for incorporating resilience principles into infrastructure investment decision processes. For instance, the first condition enhancing implementation of the guidelines—

Table 3.2
Summary of Lessons Learned from Implementing the Infrastructure Resilience Guidelines and Potential Primary Actors

	Stakeholders with Primary Role in Addressing Each Lesson			
	Federal Government	State Government	Local Government	Consultants, Contractors, Professional Organizations, or Nongovernmental Organizations
Lessons learned from conditions that facilitated implementation of the guidelines				
Agencies incorporate resilience principles into standard processes.	✓	✓	✓	✓
Broad federal government focus on resilience principles.	✓			
Established community vision and planning processes prior to disaster.		✓	✓	✓
Lessons learned from challenges posed by the guidelines				
Balance generality versus specificity.	✓			
Clarify and align resilience meanings and metrics.	✓	✓	✓	✓
Find appropriate and sufficient resources and expertise.	✓	✓	✓	✓
Integrate and streamline overlapping or competing requirements or needs.	✓	✓	✓	
Develop the science.	✓	✓	✓	✓

agencies incorporate resilience principles into standard processes—is best addressed by all actors because there are multiple levels of governance involved in building resilience, and each type of actor will bring in-depth knowledge of existing processes relevant to decisions within their purview. Incorporating multiple perspectives ensures that the principles are consistent with best practices. In contrast, the second condition—having broad federal government focus on resilience principles—is driven primarily by the federal government because this is the level of governance at which an overall national direction is set. The third condition—having an established community vision and planning processes prior to disaster—is of course not in the realm of the federal government, but primarily identified through a collaboration of the entities with more-local information, perspectives, and preferences. For the list of challenges posed by the guidelines, only the federal government is checked as a primary actor in balancing generality versus specificity in the guidelines because of its unique overarching perspective that considers the diverse roles and responsibilities of the many federal agencies. Primary responsibility for the other challenges is more distributed across multiple actors because these challenges need multilevel responses, including top-down and bottom-up approaches.

CHAPTER FOUR

Applying the Infrastructure Resilience Guidelines to Nonrecovery Environments

Infrastructure resilience is important to consider not only after a disaster but also throughout the life cycle of infrastructure systems. A series of decisions during construction and operation (e.g., regarding location, design, and funding) contributes to the long-term service and safety of infrastructure. Making decisions in the context of a common resilience framework is viewed as a best practice for improving national infrastructure resilience. To address the question of whether the Infrastructure Resilience Guidelines could be applied in nonrecovery environments, we asked interviewees to consider the potential value and feasibility of using the guidelines beyond decisions about Sandy supplemental funds. Specifically, we asked interviewees to discuss opportunities or challenges that they thought might be encountered if the guidelines were implemented for decisionmaking about federal funds for infrastructure in a nondisaster context. We learned that interviewees were enthusiastic about applying the resilience principles in the guidelines broadly, once the challenges mentioned earlier are addressed. We also learned that interviewees emphasized the need for in-depth consideration of whether the guidelines require additional modification for nonrecovery contexts and how the guidelines complement a comprehensive strategy for improving resilience nationally.

Support for Considering the Broader Application of the Guidelines

In general, interviewees were enthusiastic about resilience concepts being applied to infrastructure investment decisions and supported the broader application of the guidelines, once the challenges described in Chapter Three are addressed. One particular attraction is that broader application would encourage more-holistic or systems-level thinking (e.g., adopting a watershed approach). Interviewees reported that one benefit of adopting a systems approach is that it helps a project gain momentum with a wider variety of stakeholders and potentially attract longer-term support for infrastructure projects. A systems approach also encourages agencies to change their policies on how they invest in their own capital improvement funding.

Applying the guidelines in a nonrecovery context would elevate the focus on resilience to standard operating procedure for federal agencies. Some interviewees noted that it may be appropriate to have the guidelines apply only to projects of a certain size (e.g., greater than $50 million) so as not to unduly burden smaller projects.

A Need to Consider a Comprehensive Strategy for Achieving Greater Resilience

Though there was no real opposition to the notion of applying the guidelines in a nonrecovery context, some interviewees thought the guidelines might require modifications to be effective and applicable in nonrecovery environments. Other interviewees questioned whether applying this specific set of guidelines more broadly was the best approach to achieving national resilience. They noted that the existing guidelines were developed under significant time constraints and in the wake of Hurricane Sandy. Some interviewees suggested that perhaps we should not be asking whether these guidelines could be applied more broadly. Rather, to achieve greater resilience in the future—especially in a nonrecovery environment—we should be asking, "What is the best way to meet that goal?" That is, a more comprehensive, broader consultation with stakeholders and consideration of current (and pending) efforts to increase infrastructure resilience in broad ways (e.g., not just through implementing the existing guidelines, but by developing science-based standards) might lead to a more effective resilience initiative. If the starting question is how to improve national resilience, the federal government may be better served by thinking about resilience more comprehensively and effectively. That is, the guidelines would be one complementary part of a broader comprehensive resilience strategy.

Several interviewees emphasized that, without a change in requirements (e.g., as occurred with the Sandy Recovery and Improvement Act), it may be very difficult to implement the guidelines because extra resilience efforts are not as well funded. That is, after a disaster, additional funding flows to the area for which resilience efforts can be supported, but without a disaster, there will not be additional dollars for resilience efforts. Because addressing such issues as profound uncertainty (e.g., about future precipitation conditions) adds cost to projects, some interviewees questioned whether the guidelines would be implemented if they were not tied to billions of dollars of resilience funding. In short, community motivation or incentive is likely lower in the absence of a disaster and additional funding linked with that disaster. In nonrecovery contexts, it may be helpful to consider conditions that enhance understanding and acceptance of increased short-term costs as an important means to reducing long-term costs.

Interviewees also emphasized that identifying hazard-specific challenges will be important in nonrecovery contexts. For instance, how do the challenges posed by wildfires, earthquakes, tornadoes, and river flooding differ from hurricane disasters? Moreover, each disaster and each community will be characterized by different impacts. If a statutory or regulatory change is to be made, then full consideration of the implications will be needed to determine whom the guidelines apply to, how they apply, and how affordable it is to meet them.

Similarly, questions need to be clarified about exactly what infrastructure the guidelines would be applied to (e.g., all infrastructure or only federal infrastructure, new construction, or critical infrastructure)? Furthermore, what would trigger the implementation of the guidelines, and would existing infrastructure need to be brought up to a certain standard?

To implement guidelines in a nondisaster setting, it will be necessary in some cases to consider whether and how to align existing agency authorities with resilience objectives. For instance, FTA, under emergency rule authority, has the discretion to waive certain requirements in an emergency. The interim final rule for the Emergency Relief Program lays out the approach to be adopted postevent so that work can be undertaken promptly to help a community get back up and running (see FTA, 2013b). The interim final rule is categorically excluded from the environmental assessments required by the National Environmental Policy Act. Without such exclusions, additional (sometimes lengthy) assessment processes would be required before a project receives approval.

More broadly, however, while regulatory and administrative process relief may help communities recover and rebuild quickly, it is also possible that such relief can contribute to decisions that are not aligned with resiliency principles (e.g., because immediate needs following a disaster are prioritized over long-term goals). If a vision is developed in advance and yields standards that can be applied to recovery efforts in an expedited way, then relaxing some standard processes might lead to quicker recovery and greater resiliency. In the absence of advanced planning, coordination, and development of standards, however, relaxing standard processes may yield contrary results.

Summary of Considerations in Applying the Guidelines to Nonrecovery Environments

Assuming that the challenges noted in Chapter Three are addressed, we found enthusiasm for the spirit of the resilience principles and general support for a broader application of the guidelines. In addition, interviewees suggested that the guidelines could be complemented with more in-depth consideration by the federal government about alternative strategies for achieving resilience. There may also be some circumstances that are unique to recovery environments, thus limiting the effectiveness of a broader application of the guidelines.

CHAPTER FIVE

Findings and Conclusions

To be resilient, regions need to withstand the effects of a disaster, respond effectively, recover quickly, adapt to changing conditions, and manage future disaster risk. Following the havoc wreaked on the East Coast of the United States by Hurricane Sandy in 2012, a presidential task force developed the Infrastructure Resilience Guidelines to ensure that federal agencies incorporate key principles of resilience into their formulation, evaluation, and prioritization of infrastructure investments (see Hurricane Sandy Rebuilding Task Force, 2013a). The seven principles in the guidelines are described at a general level and were released after some of the Sandy supplemental funding was already allocated. For this study, we interviewed a diverse range of public- and private-sector representatives and reviewed documents to examine whether and how the guidelines have been implemented, what lessons have been learned, and whether the same guidelines could be implemented more broadly.

The Infrastructure Resilience Guidelines Reflect Worthy Resilience Principles, but Some Challenges Need to Be Addressed

Our analysis indicates that, overall, most of those we interviewed believed that the Infrastructure Resilience Guidelines reflect worthy resiliency principles that merit pursuing more broadly, not just in a recovery context. The guidelines evidently reinforced the approach to resilience principles that many agencies had been pursuing in recent years. Rebuilding structures and systems to more resilient standards to better withstand future storms was not a new concept to most of the federal agencies represented by our interviewees. While there is typically not a one-to-one match between agencies' existing resilience principles and the guidelines, a crosswalk between the two often revealed that there was enough significant overlap that existing principles could be followed, though perhaps with slight modifications. A broad federal focus on building resilience, including a range of previous guidelines, frameworks, requirements, plans, and executive orders, appears to have stimulated a culture of resilience across agencies such that implementing the guidelines did not pose a significant challenge for most of the agencies we interviewed. For those agencies or grantees that did not have existing resilience principles, the guidelines challenged their thinking and procedures, particularly related to promoting a systems-level approach to rebuilding and promoting green infrastructure to address flooding and other storm impacts.

Additionally, jurisdictions that had already established a community plan or vision prior to Hurricane Sandy found it easier to prioritize longer-term results over solving immediate needs. Immediately following a disaster, urgent needs and stress are likely to demand the most attention, with the long-term vision understandably receiving less attention. However, jurisdictions that had already established a good understanding of resilience and had identified data on communities and structures at risk were more efficient in putting the Sandy supplemental funds to work.

The timing of the release of the guidelines did present challenges. Some agencies had already allocated funding and/or issued internal guidance requiring integration of resiliency and sustainability principles into their efforts by the time the guidelines were developed and, therefore, did not have the opportunity to apply them. It should also be noted that many infrastructure projects are only now just beginning, so to the extent that these guidelines are not just planned for but are actually implemented is not yet known. Some interviewees observed that promoting resilience principles seems important but that compliance with the guidelines is difficult to measure and enforce. This assessment is more straightforward for the portion of Sandy supplemental funds that were distributed through RFPs that incorporated the guidelines. Furthermore, determining the effect of the guidelines on infrastructure resilience will not be possible in the short term, but a long-term evaluation process should be undertaken.

Interviewees noted several other challenges. One key difficulty was finding the right balance in the guidelines between providing guidance that is broad enough to be relevant to all agencies and missions but that is also specific enough to allow agencies to determine when a guideline has been met. Providing ranges of methods or metrics for each of the guidelines may facilitate compliance.

Another challenge interviewees noted was finding appropriate and sufficient resources and expertise to implement the guidelines. For instance, implementing some of the principles in the guidelines might be beyond the expertise of some community development staff at the state or city level, and some grantees needed help understanding that they may be able to draw from existing studies. Some jurisdictions and grantees reported also that integrating diverse data sets and developing a systemwide plan with regional collaboration was a challenge, and they often lacked staff with the relevant substantive knowledge or available time to carry out this work. Although different variables from different sources are increasingly available for systems-level analyses, such an approach requires specialized knowledge and training and additional resources such as staff time and computing facilities to do effectively. State and city agencies relying more heavily on their federal colleagues with technical expertise required additional resources, as did the new role of providing a greater level of federal scrutiny.

To cope with the increasing number of resilience initiatives at various levels of government, interviewees expressed a strong desire for a more streamlined approach to complying with the myriad guidance, executive orders, frameworks, and plans related to resilience. There is significant overlap among various sets of guidelines, and, apart from regulatory requirements and agency mission, which take primacy, there is no guidance on prioritizing or differentiating across these sets of guidelines. Groups working on new guidelines that apply more broadly should minimize redundancy by streamlining these requirements.

Efforts to better develop the scientific underpinnings of the effects of these resilience projects will lead to better decisionmaking about how best to deploy resilience dollars in the future. NIST's work on developing building codes and standards that reflect increased resilience will provide one new evidence-based approach, as will DOI's plan to conduct a third-party evaluation on the suite of resilience projects it funded using its Coastal Resilience Conservation Framework. They will assess which projects actually increased resilience and how the projects contributed to a regional resilience.

A More Comprehensive Consideration of How to Improve National Resilience May Be Needed

Importantly, some interviewees questioned whether simply applying the existing guidelines to a nonrecovery context was the best approach to improving resilience. Rather, a more comprehensive and in-depth consultation of stakeholders about how to improve national resilience (e.g., by developing science-based standards) might prove more effective in the long term. This initial assessment of the implementation of the guidelines was not designed to determine if alternative approaches would have produced more-effective outcomes, but further research could address this question. For instance, what is the relative effectiveness of national implementation of the guidelines versus a nationwide implementation of a regional coordination approach, floodplain, or other standard? Another way to approach this question might be to search for robust commonalities across agencies that chose to modify existing programs (instead of developing new programs) to distribute Sandy supplemental funds. Such information would speak to important considerations when deciding the most-suitable approaches in the future.

The guidelines also should be studied more closely in anticipation of other contexts. For example, when working under a presidential disaster declaration, some agencies receive regulatory and administrative process relief to recover and rebuild as quickly as possible. These conditions would not exist outside of a disaster declaration. However, it is possible that relief from some regulatory and administrative processes can contribute to decisions that are not aligned with resiliency principles, especially if there is little or no advanced planning, coordination, and development of standards.

Additional Questions for Further Research

Additional research might provide important detail on several other questions raised by this initial assessment. First, are there systematic differences across agencies in how they attempted to meet each principle in the guidelines? A robust response to this question would require representative sampling of interviewees from each agency and use of a structured questionnaire to capture measures that are comparable across agencies. Second, are some of the principles in the guidelines easier than others to implement, and what evidence-based strategies address the challenges identified? For instance, incorporating projections of future climatic conditions seems to be one of the harder resilience principles to address, but there is a growing body of research suggesting that scenario planning methods may help decisionmakers to characterize uncertainty and to think through plausible futures in a robust way (Mahmoud et al., 2009). Additional studies would help to clarify which scenario methods are most effective in which decision context.

Further research might also examine whether applying the guidelines in a nondisaster context could affect the cost of investing. For instance, research could address whether public-private investment partnerships might be discouraged if the federal government applied the guidelines in various contexts. Additional research could examine how the budget community could be connected better with the capital asset planning community.

Finally, determining the effectiveness of the guidelines in building long-term resilience requires agencies to conceptualize their expectations of how change in resilience occurs and then to identify and monitor multiple metrics to evaluate the accuracy of those expectations over time. Theory-based program evaluation research will be useful to support this endeavor (e.g., developing and testing an action-logic model; Funnell and Rogers, 2011). One potentially informative approach would be to collect information about how each agency implements each principle in the guidelines and then to trace how grantees make subsequent decisions (and the results of those decisions) as projects are completed, analyzing both quantitative and qualitative metrics of the effectiveness of the guidelines in increasing infrastructure resilience and other outcomes achieved.

APPENDIX A

Semistructured Interview Protocol

The following questions provided guidance for topics to cover during the semistructured interviews. Not all questions were used for all interviewees; we selected only the questions that were relevant in each interview.

1. Describe how your agency used the Infrastructure Resilience Guidelines as part of recovery planning.
2. What other agencies or grantees should be interviewed for this study?
3. What were the barriers to (or limitations in) using the guidelines?
4. How have the guidelines had an impact?
5. How did the guidelines affect recovery?
6. What, if any, modifications or improvements would you suggest for the guidelines?
7. Did you identify any gaps in the guidelines in either the implementation or receipt of guidance?
8. How are agencies/recipients of funding measuring the effectiveness of the guidelines?
9. How have the guidelines changed the ways in which federal money is spent on infrastructure resilience (compared with previous recovery efforts)?
10. How was the guidance to incorporate the guidelines communicated to stakeholders? How effective was the communication?
11. What are the biggest challenges to incorporating the guidelines for Sandy recovery?

12. What are the biggest challenges to incorporating the guidelines beyond Sandy recovery?
13. What tools/resources/data/information do stakeholders need to implement guidelines?
14. Would you recommend applying the guidelines to other recovery situations? Why or why not?
15. Would the guidelines be effective for nondisaster decisionmaking—for instance, informing federal infrastructure investment decisions?
16. What second-order effects of investments in rebuilding did you identify (e.g., subcontracting requirements)?
17. Are there alternative means to accomplish the same goals that the guidelines seek to achieve (e.g., building code modifications, zoning alterations)?
18. How might the guidelines be used to encourage a "culture of resilience"?

APPENDIX B

Detailed Methods

Participants

We conducted 31 individual and small-group interviews by telephone with a total of 67 individuals from July 7 to September 19, 2014. Interviewees were selected to reflect a diverse range of organization types, decisionmaker perspectives, and sectors. The sample included 48 individuals from 14 federal departments or agencies and 19 individuals from ten state and local governments and nongovernmental organizations, about 71 percent of which received Sandy supplemental funds for infrastructure projects. We included organizations that did not receive funds because, regardless of the Sandy supplemental, their missions and responsibilities indicated that they may have relevant perspectives on developing the guidelines, incorporating resilience parameters into allocation of federal funding, and building infrastructure resilience. Interviewees included high-level decisionmakers (e.g., directors) through to operational staff (e.g., project leaders) from various sectors, including planning, urban development, security, health, environment, commerce, insurance, science standards, engineering, technology, and transport. Interviewees were located primarily in New York, New Jersey, Virginia, and the District of Columbia.

Approach

We recruited interviewees using a purposive sampling technique with the goal of obtaining a diverse sample representing a range of organizational types (federal and nonfederal organizations), perspectives (received funding, did not receive funding), and sectors (e.g., planning, urban development, security). Interviewees were initially recruited via members of the Critical Infrastructure Security and Resilience Interagency Policy Committee's Subcommittee on Recovery and Mitigation. The Subcommittee identified relevant points of contact within its agencies of people who were most knowledgeable about the process of managing Sandy supplemental funds, about implementing the guidelines or similar principles, and about resilience initiatives broadly. We emailed invitations to participate in the study to the identified individuals directly or via the agency points of contact, with at least two follow-up invitations by email or telephone to nonrespondents. We used a snowball approach to identify other relevant individuals (based on the recommendations of initial participants) who might provide important information.

A semistructured interview protocol (see Appendix A) guided discussions with interviewees. We asked about how the Infrastructure Resilience Guidelines have been used in different contexts, whether any challenges were encountered during implementation, how the guidelines were communicated, and whether it would be feasible to apply the guidelines to nonrecovery environments. The average length of the interviews was 41 minutes. We also reviewed documents relevant to the implementation of the guidelines (e.g., RFPs incorporating resilience principles) and used a keywords-in-context technique (Tesch, 1990) to identify qualitative themes in interview notes and documents. A summary of themes was reached by consensus between two of the report's authors.

Federal Departments and Agencies That Participated in Developing the Infrastructure Resilience Guidelines

To develop the Infrastructure Resilience Guidelines, representatives from the following departments and agencies participated in working group meetings and the data call on preexisting grant and direct investment programs: Council for Environmental Quality, Department of

Energy, DHS National Protection and Programs Directorate Office of Infrastructure Protection, DOI, DOT, EPA, FEMA, General Services Administration, HUD, NOAA, and USACE.

Data Quality

We ensured high-quality data by addressing four main factors:

- *Heterogeneity and diversity* was assessed by looking across multiple data sources, such as
  - insider versus outsider perspectives (including individuals from federal and nonfederal organizations)
  - micro versus macro perspectives (including directors/leaders and operational/project staff)
  - different organizational types and roles (including organizations that received funding and those that participated in planning or observed the process but did not receive funding).
- *Confirmability* was assessed, where possible, by verifying statements against documents (e.g., Were the guidelines reflected in *Federal Register* notices, RFPs, policy memos, and our interviews?).
- *Credibility* was assessed frequently during our interviews by checking respondents' agreement with paraphrasings of their comments, to ensure accurate representation of what was said in the interviews.
- *Trustworthiness* was assessed by asking knowledgeable others (e.g., subcommittee members) to corroborate the responses.

APPENDIX C

Sample Grantees

Sample HUD Grantees

The state of New York has used its CDBG funding to address housing needs, encourage economic development, and establish the Community Reconstruction Program, among other activities. The Community Reconstruction Program allows those communities severely damaged by Hurricane Sandy to identify resilient and innovative reconstruction projects based on community-driven plans that consider current damage, future threats, and the communities' economic opportunities. To apply, communities develop recovery plans and submit them to the state.

New York City has passed 16 pieces of legislation related to changes to the building code for increasing resilience and adopting best practices (City of New York, 2014). For properties in the 100-year floodplain facing increased flood risk, the city is also launching an incentive program to adopt Core Flood Resiliency Measures and plans to track the number of buildings that adopt the measures as a metric.

Sample DOI Grantees

The City of Norfolk, Virginia, received an NFWF grant to develop a green infrastructure master plan, finalize a coastal flooding study of the Lafayette River watershed, and initiate eight living shoreline projects. Norfolk has been thinking about resiliency, particularly the coastal flooding impacts, as a result of a nor'easter (a large-scale storm) that hit in 2008, but the NFWF grant challenged Norfolk to develop a more systematic, larger-scale, and longer-term approach to resilience. The first six years of the city's resiliency efforts focused on stormwater and how to keep the water out, but it is now considering other systems that might be affected by a storm and how to adapt to those changes.

Another NFWF grantee, the American Littoral Society, is a conservation organization based in New Jersey that received funding shortly after Hurricane Sandy to conduct a rapid assessment of the storm's impact on habitats from the Delaware Bay to the Long Island Sound and then to carry out a habitat restoration project. In collaboration with Rutgers University, the organization used satellite imagery to assess land-use changes and conducted a series of interviews with resource managers, park managers, and other wildlife managers as part of the assessment. The assessment identified the Delaware Bayshore as an area in need of immediate habitat restoration. This habitat is a site for horseshoe crabs and migratory birds. NFWF and others used this assessment in developing funding plans.

NFWF provided funding to the American Littoral Society to participate in the immediate habitat restoration of the Delaware Bayshore. The organization helped coordinate the federal agency response (designing the habitat response plan, establishing permit procedures, working with contractors carrying out the work, and interacting with local communities) so that everyone involved was contributing very efficiently under the limited time frame. As a result, the team was able to restore almost six miles of beaches and 50 acres of wetlands between January and the spring of 2013, in time for the horseshoe crab mating season. The American Littoral Society received an additional grant through an NFWF grant competition to build on the Delaware Bay habitat restoration project that focuses more on building resiliency along the shoreline. For this grant, it needed to meet the criteria in the NFWF solicitation that required describing how the project would promote resilience, as well as a focus on green infrastructure, regional collaboration, and other principles reflected in the Infrastructure Resilience Guidelines.

References

American Society of Civil Engineers, *Guiding Principles for the Nation's Critical Infrastructure*, Reston, Va., 2009. As of November 17, 2014:
http://www.asce.org/uploadedFiles/Issues_and_Advocacy/Our_Initiatives/Infrastructure/Content_Pieces/critical-infrastructure-guiding-principles-report.pdf

City of New York, *A Stronger, More Resilient New York*, PlaNYC, NYC Special Initiative for Rebuilding and Resiliency, New York, June 11, 2013. As of September 24, 2014:
http://www.nyc.gov/html/sirr/html/report/report.shtml

———, *Progress Report 2014: A Greener, Greater New York, A Stronger, More Resilient New York*, PlaNYC, New York, April 22, 2014. As of October 22, 2014:
http://www.nyc.gov/html/planyc/downloads/pdf/140422_PlaNYCP-Report_FINAL_Web.pdf

DHS—*See* U.S. Department of Homeland Security.

DOI—*See* U.S. Department of the Interior.

DOT—*See* U.S. Department of Transportation.

Executive Office of the President, "Federal Leadership in Environmental, Energy, and Economic Performance," Executive Order 13514, October 5, 2009. As of September 24, 2014:
http://www.whitehouse.gov/administration/eop/ceq/sustainability

———, "National Preparedness," Presidential Policy Directive 8, March 30, 2011. As of October 15, 2014:
http://www.dhs.gov/presidential-policy-directive-8-national-preparedness

———, "Critical Infrastructure Security and Resilience," Presidential Policy Directive 21, February 12, 2013a. As of October 15, 2014:
http://www.whitehouse.gov/the-press-office/2013/02/12/presidential-policy-directive-critical-infrastructure-security-and-resil

———, *The President's Climate Action Plan*, Washington, D.C., June 2013b. As of September 24, 2014:
http://www.whitehouse.gov/sites/default/files/image/president27sclimateactionplan.pdf

———, "Preparing the United States for the Impacts of Climate Change," Executive Order 13653, November 1, 2013c. As of September 24, 2014:
http://www.whitehouse.gov/the-press-office/2013/11/01/executive-order-preparing-united-states-impacts-climate-change

EOP—*See* Executive Office of the President.

Federal Emergency Management Agency, *Consideration of Environmental Benefits in the Evaluation of Acquisition Projects Under the Hazard Mitigation Assistance (HMA) Programs*, Mitigation Policy FP-108-024-01, June 18, 2013. As of September 24, 2014:
http://www.fema.gov/media-library-data/20130726-1920-25045-4319/environmental_benefits_policy_june_18_2013_mitigation_policy_fp_108_024_01.pdf

———, *Minimum Design Standards for Hazard Mitigation Assistance Projects in Flood Hazard Areas*, Mitigation Policy 203-074-1, April 21, 2014. As of September 24, 2014:
http://www.fema.gov/media-library-data/1398192935992-150e892546cec441ec6f961a023f2cce/Signed%20ASCE-24-05%20Policy.pdf

Federal Transit Administration, "Availability of Emergency Relief Funds in Response to Hurricane Sandy," *Federal Register*, Vol. 78, No. 25, February 6, 2013a, pp. 8691–8698. As of September 24, 2014:
http://www.gpo.gov/fdsys/pkg/FR-2013-02-06/pdf/2013-02729.pdf

———, "Allocation of Public Transportation Emergency Relief Funds in Response to Hurricane Sandy," *Federal Register*, Vol. 78, No. 61, March 29, 2013b, pp. 19357–19362. As of September 24, 2014:
https://federalregister.gov/a/2013-07268

———, "Second Allocation of Public Transportation Emergency Relief Funds in Response to Hurricane Sandy: Response, Recovery, and Resiliency," *Federal Register*, Vol. 78, No. 103, May 29, 2013c, pp. 32296–32302. As of September 24, 2014:
http://www.gpo.gov/fdsys/pkg/FR-2013-05-29/pdf/2013-12766.pdf

———, "Funding Availability for Resilience Projects in Response to Hurricane Sandy," *Federal Register*, Vol. 78, No. 248, December 26, 2013d, pp. 78486–78493. As of September 24, 2014:
http://www.gpo.gov/fdsys/pkg/FR-2013-12-26/pdf/2013-30867.pdf

FEMA—*See* Federal Emergency Management Agency.

FTA—*See* Federal Transit Administration.

Funnell, S. C., and P. J. Rogers, *Purposeful Program Theory: Effective Use of Theories of Change and Logic Models*, San Francisco: Wiley, 2011.

HUD—*See* U.S. Department of Housing and Urban Development.

Hurricane Sandy Rebuilding Task Force, *Hurricane Sandy Rebuilding Strategy: Stronger Communities, a Resilient Region*, August 2013a. As of September 24, 2014: http://portal.hud.gov/hudportal/documents/huddoc?id=hsrebuildingstrategy.pdf

———, "Infrastructure Resilience Guidelines Webinar," August 2013b. As of November 3, 2014:
http://www.youtube.com/watch?v=t71i4m_O0DQ

Kousky, Carolyn, and Leonard Shabman, "A New Era of Disaster Aid? Reflections on the Sandy Supplemental," Issue Brief 13-05, Washington, D.C.: Resources for the Future, December 2013. As of October 22, 2014:
http://www.rff.org/RFF/Documents/RFF-IB-13-05.pdf

Mahmoud, M., et al., "A Formal Framework for Scenario Development in Support of Environmental Decision-Making," *Environmental Modeling & Software*, Vol. 24, 2009, pp. 798–808.

Munich Re, *Severe Weather in North America: Perils, Risks, Insurance*, Executive Summary, Munich, Germany: Münchener Rückversicherungs-Gesellschaft, 2012. As of October 21, 2014:
http://www.munichreamerica.com/site/mram/get/documents_E1449378742/mram/assetpool.mr_america/PDFs/3_Publications/ks_severe_weather_na_exec_summary.pdf

National Climatic Data Center, "Billion-Dollar Weather/Climate Disasters," web page, no date. As of September 24, 2014:
http://www.ncdc.noaa.gov/billions

National Fish and Wildlife Foundation, "Hurricane Sandy Coastal Resiliency Competitive Grant Program," New York, 2013. As of September 24, 2014:
http://www.nfwf.org/hurricanesandy/Documents/Hurricane%20Sandy%20Fact%20Sheet.pdf

———, "2013 Hurricane Sandy Coastal Resiliency Competitive Grants Program RFP," January 31, 2014. As of September 24, 2014:
http://www.nfwf.org/hurricanesandy/Pages/2013rfp.aspx

National Oceanic and Atmospheric Administration, "FY 2013 Disaster Relief Appropriations Act for Coastal Resilience Networks," Federal Funding Opportunity No. NOAA-NOS-CSC-2013-2003866, August 28, 2013. As of September 24, 2014:
http://coast.noaa.gov/funding/_pdf/NOAA-NOS-CSC-2013-2003866%20Coastal%20Resilience%20DRA%20funding%20posted%2008.28.2013%20closing%2009.30.2013.pdf?redirect=301ocm

National Oceanic and Atmospheric Administration and U.S. Army Corps of Engineers, "Infrastructure Systems Rebuilding Principles," February 28, 2013. As of September 24, 2014:
http://coastalmanagement.noaa.gov/resources/docs/infsysrebuildingprinciples.pdf

NFWF—*See* National Fish and Wildlife Foundation.

NOAA—*See* National Oceanic and Atmospheric Administration.

NOAA and USACE—*See* National Oceanic and Atmospheric Administration and U.S. Army Corps of Engineers.

Pielke, Roger A., Jr., Joel Gratz, Christopher W. Landsea, Douglas Collins, Mark A. Saunders, and Rade Musulin, "Normalized Hurricane Damage in the United States: 1900–2005," *Natural Hazards Review*, Vol. 9, No. 1, February 2008, pp. 29–42.

Sawyers, Andrew, and Peter C. Grevatt, "Award of Capitalization Grants with Funds Appropriated by P.L. 113-2, the 'Disaster Relief Appropriations Act,'" Memorandum to Joan L. Matthews, Region II, U.S. Environmental Protection Agency, May 1, 2013.

Tesch, Renata, *Qualitative Research: Analysis Types and Software Tools,* New York: Falmer, 1990.

U.S. Army Corps of Engineers, *First Interim Report: Disaster Relief Appropriations Act, 2013*, March 11, 2013a. As of September 24, 2014:
http://www.nad.usace.army.mil/Portals/40/docs/Sandy Related Docs/First_Interim_Report.pdf

———, *Second Interim Report: Disaster Relief Appropriations Act, 2013*, May 30, 2013b. As of September 24, 2014:
http://www.usace.army.mil/Portals/2/docs/Emergency%20Ops/Second_Interim_Report_FINAL.pdf

———, *Hurricane Sandy Coastal Projects Performance Evaluation Study: Disaster Relief Appropriations Act, 2013*, November 6, 2013c. As of September 24, 2014:
http://www.nan.usace.army.mil/About/Hurricane_Sandy/CoastalProjectsPerformanceEvaluationStudy.aspx

U.S. Department of Homeland Security, *National Infrastructure Protection Plan 2013: Partnering for Critical Infrastructure Security and Resilience*, Washington, D.C., 2013a. As of October 15, 2014:
http://www.dhs.gov/sites/default/files/publications/NIPP%202013_Partnering%20for%20Critical%20Infrastructure%20Security%20and%20Resilience_508_0.pdf

———, *National Mitigation Framework*, Washington, D.C., 2013b. As of September 24, 2014:
http://www.fema.gov/media-library-data/20130726-1914-25045-9956/final_national_mitigation_framework_20130501.pdf

U.S. Department of Housing and Urban Development, "Allocations, Common Application, Waivers, and Alternative Requirements for Grantees Receiving Community Development Block Grant (CDBG) Disaster Recovery Funds in Response to Hurricane Sandy," *Federal Register*, Vol. 78, No. 43, March 5, 2013a, pp. 14329–14349. As of September 24, 2014:
http://www.gpo.gov/fdsys/pkg/FR-2013-03-05/pdf/2013-05170.pdf

———, "Clarifying Guidance, Waivers, and Alternative Requirements for Hurricane Sandy Grantees in Receipt of Community Development Block Grant Disaster Recovery Funds," *Federal Register*, Vol. 78, No. 76, April 19, 2013b, pp. 23578–23581. As of September 24, 2014:
http://www.gpo.gov/fdsys/pkg/FR-2013-04-19/pdf/2013-09228.pdf

———, "Allocations, Waivers, and Alternative Requirements for Grantees Receiving Community Development Block Grant Disaster Recovery Funds in Response to Disasters Occurring in 2011 or 2012," *Federal Register*, Vol. 78, No. 103, May 29, 2013c, pp. 32262–32269. As of September 24, 2014:
http://www.gpo.gov/fdsys/pkg/FR-2013-05-29/pdf/2013-12683.pdf

———, "Second Allocation, Waivers, and Alternative Requirements for Grantees Receiving Community Development Block Grant (CDBG) Disaster Recovery Funds in Response to Hurricane Sandy," *Federal Register*, Vol. 78, No. 222, November 18, 2013d, p. 69104. As of September 24, 2014:
http://www.gpo.gov/fdsys/pkg/FR-2013-11-18/pdf/2013-27506.pdf

———, "Second Allocation, Waivers, and Alternative Requirements for Grantees Receiving Community Development Block Grant (CDBG) Disaster Recovery Funds in Response to Disasters Occurring in 2013," *Federal Register*, Vol. 78, No. 222, November 18, 2014. As of September 24, 2014:
http://www.gpo.gov/fdsys/pkg/FR-2013-11-18/html/2013-27506.htm

U.S. Department of the Interior, *Hurricane Sandy Disaster Relief Supplemental Appropriations Spending Plan*, Washington, D.C., 2013. As of September 24, 2014:
http://www.doi.gov/news/pressreleases/upload/2013_05_06-hurricane-sandy-plan-sm.pdf

U.S. Department of Transportation, *Climate Adaptation Plan: Ensuring Transportation Infrastructure and System Resilience*, Washington, D.C., 2013. As of September 24, 2014:
http://www.dot.gov/sites/dot.dev/files/docs/DOT%20Adaptation%20Plan.pdf

Wright, Roy E., "Sea Level Rise and Hazard Mitigation Assistance Programs," Memorandum, Washington, D.C.: Federal Emergency Management Agency, December 23, 2013. As of September 24, 2014:
http://www.fema.gov/media-library/assets/documents/89659